Peoples of the Rain Forest

Robert Low

FRANKLIN WATTS
NEW YORK • LONDON • SYDNEY

This edition first published in the UK in 1997 by
Franklin Watts
96 Leonard Street
London
EC2A 4RH

© 1996 The Rosen Publishing Group, Inc., New York

Picture credits: Cover © Eliot Elisofon/Eliot Elisofon Photographic Archives,
National Museum of African Art, Smithsonian Institution; pp 4, 12, 20
© Bertrand Rieger/Gamma Liaison; p. 7 © Wendy Stone/Gamma Liaison;
pp. 8, 15 © Dr Colin M. Turnbull, Joseph Allen Towles Collection,
Avery Research Center for African American History & Culture; p. 11 © Pat Zelt/ANAKO
Editions; p. 16 © Pacific Pictures-John Penisten/Liaison International; p. 19 © Lam Duc/ANAKO Editions.

A CIP catalogue record for this book is available from the British Library.

ISBN 0 7496 2863 4

Printed in the United States of America

Contents

What is a rain forest?

A rain forest is a forest that grows in an area that is warm all year round and has lots of rain. There are rain forests in many parts in the world. Most of them are in **tropical** areas.

The trees in rain forests grow very close together. This means that little light reaches the ground. But many plants and animals live in rain forests.

◀ Rain forests have a great variety of plants and animals living in them.

Peoples of the rain forest

Many different peoples live in the world's rain forests. For example, the **Mbuti** live in the Ituri rain forest in central Africa. The **Huaorani** live in the Amazon rain forest in South America. And the **Dayak** live in the rain forest of Borneo, an island in South-east Asia.

These peoples live in different places and speak different languages. But because they all live in rain forests, they have many things in common.

The Mbuti live in the Ituri ▶
rain forest in Africa.

6

Living in the rain forest

Many people who live in rain forests move from place to place to hunt and grow their food. When they move to a new place, they cut down the trees and burn them. This helps make the soil **fertile** and lets in sunlight so food crops can grow.

Many of the rain forest peoples also hunt the animals that live there.
The Mbuti hunt with spears and nets.
The Huaorani use blowguns.

◀ The Mbuti hunt with bows and arrows, as well as spears and nets.

Animals and plants

The rain forest is home to many animals, from the birds and monkeys that live in the treetops to the snakes and insects on the ground.

In the Ituri rain forest there are elephants and gorillas. Wild pigs live in the Amazon, and on Borneo there are rhinoceros and deer.

Some of the plants in rain forests help people to get better when they are ill. Others are good to eat, while some are poisonous.

Brightly coloured macaws share the
Amazon rain forest with the Huaorani. ▶

Getting about

To travel through the rain forest people must cut paths through the thick undergrowth. This is hard work and the plants grow back quickly. So, if there are rivers, people use them, travelling in **canoes** or on rafts.

Borneo, where the Dayak live, has many mountains. The paths are steep and slippery. To cross narrow valleys more easily, the Dayak make bridges out of **bamboo**.

◀ The Dayak also use canoes to travel along the rivers of Borneo.

13

Food

The people who live in rain forests
have to find their own food. The Mbuti
hunt and fish and also collect fruit and nuts.

The Huaorani make wooden blowguns.
They kill animals by blowing poisoned darts
at them from the blowguns. They also fish
and grow **manioc** and maize.

The Dayak fish and hunt with blowguns
and spears. They also grow rice on
the mountainsides.

Rain forests provide many types ▶
of food for the people who live there.

Clothes

In tropical rain forests the weather is very warm all year round. So people living there do not need to wear many clothes.

The Mbuti wear light clothes made of flattened tree bark.

Most Huaorani children wear no clothes at all. Their parents wear a small piece of cloth wrapped around their waist.

◀ The Dayak weave cloth with pretty colours and patterns. Then they make it into clothes.

17

Building homes

Because many people who live in the rain forest move often, they live in homes that are quick and easy to build. The Mbuti and Huaorani build homes of wooden or bamboo poles covered with leaves.

The Dayak stay in one place. They build very large longhouses on stilts. The floors and walls are made of bamboo or tree bark. The roofs are **thatched** with palm leaves.

Huaorani homes are made from ▶
bamboo poles and leaves.

Families and communities

The Mbuti live in groups of 10 to 25 families. They help each other find food and build homes. Every month or so, they move to a new area of the rain forest.

Huaorani families usually live alone. They move in search of fresh ground in which to plant a garden.

The Dayak live in villages. Each village has several longhouses. Up to 50 families live in a longhouse and everyone works together.

◀ At special celebrations the Dayak wear their colourful traditional clothes.

Changing lives

Today, the people who live in the
rain forests face many changes. Large areas
of rain forest are being destroyed.
People who do not live in them are
cutting down trees and starting big farms
or cattle ranches.

The rain forests are getting smaller.
It is hard for the Mbuti to find animals to
hunt and for the Huaorani to find places
to grow food. Many Dayak still live in
longhouses, but they, too, have to share the
rain forest with outsiders.

Glossary

bamboo   A large, tree-like plant, with a strong, hollow stem.

canoe   Narrow boat made out of wood.

Dayak   A people who live in the mountainous rain forest of Borneo.

fertile   Soil in which plants and crops grow well.

Huaorani   A people who live in the Amazon rain forest of South America.

manioc   Plant with edible roots.

Mbuti   A people who live in the Ituri rain forest in Africa.

thatch   Grass or leaves packed tightly together to make a roof.

tropical   Part of the world that is warm all year round.

Index